Don't Act Like Prey!

A Guide to
Personal Leadership
for Women

Susan L. Farrell, MBA

SLF PUBLISHING · LEBANON, WI

Published by SLF Publishing, P.O. Box 172, Lebanon, WI 53047

Cover and interior design by AbandonedWest Creative, Inc.

IMPORTANT DISCLAIMER

The purpose of this book is to encourage the reader to think about his or her actions and to make changes if he or she wants to do so. It is based primarily upon the author's experiences. It is not intended to give advice. The author and SLF Publishing shall have neither liability nor responsibility to any person or entity with respect to any loss or damage caused, or alleged to have been caused, directly or indirectly, by the information contained in this book. If you do not wish to be bound by the above, you may return this book to the publisher for a full refund.

This book is possible because of the generous support of my husband, best friend, and the love of my life, Rick Gurka. Thank you, Rick, for everything!

Contents

Personal leadership:
Before you can lead others, you must lead yourself.

Foreword

IRONICALLY, I WAS first introduced to this book when Ms. Farrell contacted me to request my input as a "fact-checker" on the material. Apparently, to her my status as a clinical psychologist warranted me a level of expertise to do this for her, which came as a pleasant surprise to me. Despite my advanced degree, I've never really felt like much of an "expert" on anything, other than perhaps an expert on negotiating my way through years and years of school, writing extensive research papers, incurring large amounts of student loan debt, and stretching a student loan budget to keep a roof over my head for longer than initially anticipated. As for the rest of my life, I have always been a bit of a Jack-of-all-trades, master-of-none kind of person, most of it the result of insatiable curiosity and a relative lack of fear with regard to learning.

It was this fearlessness in learning that most influenced my choices in professional development. Currently I am a practicing clinical psychologist since the successful completion of my graduate training in 2005 and licensing examinations in 2009, although my work in the human services field predates this by at least 10 years. My work in the field has been extremely varied, including work as a social worker, a hospital extern on a psychiatric consultation team, a behavioral therapist for developmentally disabled children, a clinical intern at a state juvenile correctional facility, and both a masters- and doctoral-level clinical therapist/psychologist in private practice and public service. Graduate school was a very natural experience for me, and the gift that my psychological training has provided to me has been the ability to use my natural curiosity to develop a broad knowledge base on a number of subjects related to the human condition. My various work experiences have additionally put me in contact with a wide variety of human experiences and concerns to add to this fund of knowledge. Furthermore, intense research training has further allowed me to accumulate large amounts of information on a wide variety of topics so that relating to people as an "expert" clinician has been much easier than if I had only maintained a narrow focus on a small subject area. After all, people are varied and complex, and they look to others in the human services field to help them understand their complexities.

Therefore, when Ms. Farrell contacted me to "fact-check" for her on her topic of assertiveness, in true psychologist style, I fell back on my current level of knowledge about the topic of assertiveness and took on the task as a research project using all of my well-honed "fact-checking" skills. I immediately read her work and began digging though my own clinical resources that were relevant to her manuscript content. Also in true psychologist style, I located too many items to carry to our initial meeting. It is in the nature of a helping professional to be helpful. Really helpful. Even when help is not requested. We're also a thorough, if not slightly obsessive-compulsive, lot. As I had no interest in overwhelming or causing physical harm to Ms. Farrell, I chose to go against my nature and limited myself to fewer than five items with the intent to be helpful but not overwhelming. This was not an easy task. Psychologists are not known for brevity or self-restraint in matters of research, and we usually have really large libraries of really large books.

Following her request, Ms. Farrell and I initially met over some wonderful Italian food and wine to share thoughts and ideas and discuss points of focus. Gradually we moved her manuscript further along its developmental course while ingesting copious amounts of garlic and pasta. It was during this dinner that it was abundantly clear to me how passionate Ms. Farrell felt about her creation of this book. Her excitement throughout this meeting was palpable. Ultimately, it was also clear that she hadn't really needed my help at all, as her grasp of the subject matter was already very sound from all of the time she had spent sharing it in her public speaking engagements. Still, she took the materials that I had brought for her and began to incorporate many of the points that we had discussed over dinner.

Following this initial contact I continued to mull over the message that Ms. Farrell was trying to convey in her book. In true psychologist style, I continued to think about providing assistance to her even though it appeared that my initial contribution had been completed. Remember, we are a thorough, if not mildly obsessive-compulsive, lot who tend to be overly helpful. More specifically, I was brought to question what characteristics might make this book stand out from the rest of the vast self-help literature available these days. In my work as a clinical psychologist, I often come across many books dedicated to self-improvement, and anyone can visit any bookstore to find a wide variety of self-help literature readily available. Clients I have worked with have frequently presented in session with any number of self-help books dedicated to topics ranging from anxiety reduction to weight loss. Usually, the conversation begins with the client saying, "Say, I found this book at (insert major bookstore name here) about (insert topic here). Have you heard of it? What do you think?" Through therapeutic conversation the client is ultimately encouraged to share his or her own experiences with reading and working with the book material, as the personal experience of anything is much more important and relevant than the opinion of an "expert." Based on these conversations, it has become clear to me that the value of these materials to the people who use them appears to be twofold. First, the material shared in most self-help books helps people to initially feel less alone and more valid in their concerns. Not only do they find out that other people share their same concerns, but apparently their concern is also important enough for Mr. or Ms. Important Expert Author to have written a book about it. Second, and perhaps more importantly, these books sometimes provide an outline of specific steps to take toward the achievement of specific goals. So not only do people feel better about themselves in the first place, they may also experience an initial increase in motivation to make positive changes and pursue their dreams. They tap into the basic need for all people to continually grow, change, and evolve.

Still, while the number of self-help books is seemingly limitless and the initial rush of motivation following the purchase of one is compelling, more often than not these books are purchased, looked over, and then they set on a bookshelf or desk for an indefinite period of time, if not forever, and the true value of the material is lost. Why this happens is a bit of a mystery, because I strongly believe that people really want to grow and change in positive ways and they appreciate any guideposts offered to them in this pursuit. It could be considered that perhaps the number of self-help books that share information is limitless, but the number of these books that present their material in a user-friendly, creative, engaging manner is not. Clients have reported to me that they frequently end up feeling confused after reading such books, sometimes because the material is presented in an overly dry and clinical manner, sometimes because the steps for eliciting positive change are not clearly delineated, or sometimes because people feel more overwhelmed or intimidated with their new, large task of self-improvement. Often, people believe that change should be easy or smooth, and these books rarely address the more commonly experienced difficulties along the path of change.

It is in these points where I was initially struck by Ms. Farrell's manuscript. I have known Ms. Farrell for over ten years, and in that time I have witnessed many changes occurring in her life and her career. With the beginning of her own consulting business, SLF Consulting and Training, I have noticed a passion for self-improvement develop in her that has positively affected all areas of her life, from her career to her golf game. This was the passion that was so evident during our dinner and that has infused her writing of this book. The result of this infusion of enthusiasm has been the creation of a book that skillfully uses a creative metaphor to explain one of the more misunderstood concepts in personal development and includes supportive exercises that allow the reader to engage with the material on a personal level. Her honesty and candor regarding her own experiences with assertiveness further instill the reader with confidence about not only her expertise but also her empathic resonance with her audience.

Shortly after our initial dinner meeting Ms. Farrell contacted me again to rehash our initial ideas and verify that she was, indeed, still on the right track. At this time Ms. Farrell also asked me to write this foreword for her. Having never written a foreword before, the only obvious answer to this request was, "Of course! I'd be honored!" She took a great leap of faith with me that day, and I appreciate her courage. Following this request and in true psychologist style, I immediately began researching the topic of "What the heck is a foreword, and how does one write one?" Thankfully, there was plenty of material available at my disposal, so I now have one more data point of information in my own personal information store.

We soon met over one more lovely dinner (pub fare this time, not Italian) and exchanged thoughts and ideas. Thankfully, no more books were brought to this meeting, although Ms. Farrell was assured that her material in the newer version of her manuscript was still theoretically sound. Once again, during this meeting her enthusiasm for the material and the process of disseminating it in a book was infectious. In addition, the book was, once again, moved along on its developmental course and was one step closer to publication.

As of the writing of this foreword, I am certain that the book you have in your hand is the direct result of Ms. Farrell's passion and enthusiasm for this subject matter coupled with a strong command of the subject matter and a unique, engaging perspective. As the "fact-checker," I can assert that the material in this book is current and sound, based on the most up-to-date theoretical perspectives on assertiveness. Finally, as an "expert" in the field, I can assert that this is not going to be one of the self-help books that gathers dust on your bookshelf. You will want to return to this material as you progress in your own journey of self-development, and you will find her perspective, metaphors, and exercises extremely valuable in this regard. You will feel the enthusiasm that Ms. Farrell has poured into the creation of this book, and it will serve to increase your own motivation and commitment toward positive self-development.

It is my and Ms. Farrell's sincere wish that you experience success in your personal development, and it is my sincere wish that Ms. Farrell will continue to share her knowledge on this and other topics in years to come.

Amy Gurka, Ph.D.
Clinical Psychologist

Introduction

IF WE ARE to achieve the success we want in life, we must stand up for ourselves and speak out on our behalf. We cannot be passive. We must be assertive.

Many of us have difficulty in being assertive. This can be for many reasons. We want to be nice. We want to be liked. We do not want to cause conflict. We do not like confrontations. As girls, we were encouraged to be passive. These reasons are all understandable. However, they can also be obstacles to our success.

I was raised in the era when common wisdom was that "children should be seen and not heard." My parents believed this and took great pride in being able to take my brothers and me anywhere knowing that we would be quiet and would behave. I was also naturally shy. I am sure the two fed into each other. Most of the time I was quite passive.

I was also very stubborn, however. I think this trait, combined with having three younger brothers who loved to pick on me, gave me the strength to stand up for myself when I had to do so.

I remember a situation with my mother. I did not handle the situation assertively, but I was not completely passive, either.

When I was in elementary school, my mother wanted me to look and act like a little lady. She wanted me to wear skirts and dresses to school. I wanted to wear pants like I did at home. One winter I thought I had the answer. I told her my legs got cold walking to the school bus (true) and thought I should wear pants. Her answer? She bought me these really ugly black pants that I could wear under my skirt and take off when I got to school.

I was assertive enough to say something, but not enough to fully state what I wanted or to push the issue.

A similar situation happened when I was about 11 or 12. I was starting to develop breasts. At that time, training bras were what girls wore. (I still do not understand. Train them for what?) Some of my friends, however, wore real bras. I wanted to wear a real bra. (The fact that I really did not need any bra was beside the point.) Rather than tell my mother this, however, I said that my bras were too tight (partially true). Her answer? She bought me a larger size training bra, and when that was too big, she stitched little tucks into the sides.

It was not long after that that I decided I needed to work and buy my own clothes.

So why did I not simply tell my mother what I wanted? I think it was mostly because I did not want to hurt her feelings. I did not want a confrontation. I did not want conflict.

It is important to remember that no matter how we were raised, or what we were like as children, as adults, we can decide to change. We can decide to be assertive instead of passive.

Sometimes, rather than be assertive, we go overboard and become aggressive. This can be equally detrimental to achieving our personal and professional goals. When we are aggressive, we can destroy the relationships that mean the most to us.

This book is designed to help you view assertiveness in new ways. With a new perspective, it may be easier for you to stand up and speak out for yourself when necessary, without becoming aggressive. This book is based primarily upon my experiences and observations.

I hope this book helps you on your journey of personal leadership!

CHAPTER 01

Wildlife

THOSE OF YOU who have hiked in our national parks have probably noticed the abundance of signs and brochures warning what to do if you encounter wildlife. The park rangers are also extremely helpful in providing information.

In the Rocky Mountains, warnings commonly occur regarding black bears and mountain lions. My husband, Rick, and I have hiked in several of our national parks. The following are general recommendations that we have seen and heard over the years.

Make noise so that the animals hear you and can leave. It is not good to surprise them. When surprised, they can feel threatened. When threatened, they may attack. If they attack, it will be much worse for you than for them.

If they have not noticed you, you can detour around them. You do not have to return to your starting point. You do not have to give up your hike, your plans. Just modify your route.

If they have noticed you, stand tall and put your arms out. In other words, look big. If you are with someone, stand next to each other, not behind each other. Look big!

If you are hiking with children, hold their hands and put them between the adults. This makes everyone look bigger. More importantly, it keeps children from bolting. Running can initiate the chase response in some wild animals. To a mountain lion, a small, running child probably looks similar to a large, running rabbit.

We have also heard to talk to black bears in a calm, controlled voice. This lets the bear know that you are aware of it.

The idea behind all of this is to look threatening enough that the animal will not want to mess with you. However, you do not want to look or act so threatening that the animal decides it has to attack you before you attack it.

For example, a park ranger in Glacier National Park told of a hiker who had a black bear bite a chunk out of his shoulder. This sounds horrible until you hear the beginning of the story. The bear was on the trail, eating berries, doing what bears do. The man saw the bear on the trail, walked up to the bear, and punched it on the nose! Of course the bear fought back. I would have fought back, and I would bet you would have, also.

Throughout the years, I began to realize that the message was, "Don't act like prey." Do not quietly and cautiously slink through the woods hoping not to be noticed. Talk! Laugh! Sing! Let the animals know you are there.

If you meet an animal, do not run away. Stand your ground. Backing up slowly and detouring are also recommended. The point is, do not run like prey.

Do not be stupid, either. Do not attack. Fight back if you have to, but do not initiate the attack.

As more time passed, I realized that not acting like prey (hiding and running away) and not acting like a predator (attacking) defined being assertive.

While reading about the animals in this book, you may think of them as metaphors for passive, aggressive, and assertive behavior. If you do, please keep in mind that some animals, such as predators, are naturally aggressive. Other animals may be naturally passive, but become aggressive in certain situations. For example, most prey animals will fight to the best of their ability to escape if they are attacked.

Other animals are taught to be aggressive. Dogs are a good example. Some dogs are taught to guard and/or to attack. These dogs play a very important role in the military and some police departments.

Sometimes, though, animals learn to be aggressive because of fear or anxiety based on past experiences. Unfortunately, this can happen with people, too.

In this book I am using animals as examples of passive, aggressive, and assertive behavior. Please do not take these examples too literally. They are meant as a method to view these behaviors in a new, and perhaps less threatening, light, so that you can view your own behaviors in a different way.

CHAPTER 02

Rights and Respect

THE UNITED STATES' Declaration of Independence states: "We hold these truths to be self-evident, that all men are created equal, that they are endowed by their Creator with certain unalienable Rights, that among these are Life, Liberty, and the pursuit of Happiness."

We also have the right to be treated with respect, dignity, professionalism, and courtesy. We have the right to ask for help, to think and feel what we do, and to disagree with others. Why? Because we are human beings.

In addition, we have the right to set boundaries. Many animals create and defend territories. We have the right to create boundaries around what we consider acceptable behavior from others and around what we consider acceptable treatment of us. We have the right to defend those boundaries.

When it comes to children, we also have the responsibility to set boundaries around what is acceptable behavior for them. That is how they learn.

Remember something called the First Amendment? Freedom of speech? We also have the right to speak. Along with this is the right to be heard.

A large part of being assertive is speaking up for ourselves. It includes telling people what we think and how we feel. It also includes telling them the impact their words and actions have on us.

Remembering that people, we and others, have basic rights is a key to being assertive.

- **When we are passive, it is as though we forget that we have rights. We do not stand up for our rights. We let others take our rights away from us.**
- **When we are aggressive, it is as though we forget that others have the same rights we do. We take their rights away from them.**
- **When we are assertive, we remember that we have rights, and so do others. We balance our rights with theirs.**

Respect is the key to finding the balance between passive and aggressive behavior. It is the key to being assertive.

- **When we are passive, we do not respect our own rights. We do not respect ourselves.**
- **When we are aggressive, we do not respect the rights of others. We do not respect others.**
- **When we are assertive, we respect our own rights while respecting the rights of others. We balance our rights**

with others' rights. We respect ourselves at the same time we respect others.

When put this way, it sounds simple. So why do so many of us have difficulties in finding that balance between passive and aggressive called assertive?

There are many reasons. A major one is that we do what we are comfortable doing. We do what we have always done because it is easy, comfortable, and safe.

Of course, that brings up the old saying, "If you always do what you always did, you will get what you always got." If you like what you get, great! If not, it is time to make some changes.

The good news is that we can decide to change! We can decide to be assertive instead of passive or aggressive.

Is it easy to change? No. Change is seldom easy. If it were, everyone would do it regularly. Ask yourself this, though: How easy is it to continue living the way you are? Maybe making a change, being assertive, would be easier in the end than not making that change.

Something to remember is that major change is not immediate. Change takes time. As long as you make small, consistent, incremental changes, you are on the way to major change.

CHAPTER 03

Relationships

HOW WE ACT in our relationships reflects whether we are passive, assertive, or aggressive. Our actions may vary in different relationships.

We may be passive with some people and act like prey. We may run and hide, figuratively speaking.

We may be aggressive with other people and act like predators. We may attack them verbally when we are with them.

We may be assertive with still others and treat them with respect while respecting ourselves.

We have personal and professional relationships with dozens of people. We have to deal with a number of them each day.

It is time for a mental exercise. On the following page, list as many professional and personal relationships as you can. You may list the person's name or his/her relationship to you.

Personal relationships may include your spouse, parents, children, siblings, neighbors, teachers, the person who cuts your hair—you get the idea. Professional relationships may include your supervisor, employees, co-workers, customers, associates, suppliers, and all the others who enter your professional life.

After listing as many relationships as you can, ask yourself how assertive you are in each of these relationships. Would it be advantageous to be assertive, or assertive more consistently, in any of these relationships? If yes, place an asterisk next to the name or highlight it.

Think about these relationships and how you can improve them as you continue to read.

Table 3-1	**Relationships**	
Personal	Professional

CHAPTER 04

Communication

COMMUNICATION IS THE foundation of a relationship, professional or personal. Communication is what builds, or destroys, a relationship. How we communicate reflects whether we are being passive, aggressive, or assertive.

Passive communication may include speaking softly, speaking with hesitancy and uncertainty, giving in quickly when others disagree, and looking down rather than at the other person.

Aggressive communication may include shouting, yelling, interrupting the other person, not allowing others to speak, and disregarding what others say.

Assertive communication is when we clearly state what we think and actively listen to what the other person thinks. When we clearly state what we think, we make sure the other person understands us. Active listening means that we make a conscious effort to truly understand the other person. This may mean asking questions to clarify that we do understand.

When we think of communication, we usually think of talking to someone face to face. However, there are many other methods of communication. We talk on the phone, one on one, and in conference calls. We communicate in writing through letters, memos, email, and texts. We communicate every time we participate in social media.

We need to be aware of all our communication. The advantage of face to face communication is that our body language enhances and clarifies our words or contradicts them. Often our facial expressions and our body communicate more than our words do.

When we communicate by phone, our voice inflections give cues to our true meaning. The same words can take on entirely different meanings when they are said in seriousness and when they are said in jest. Although voice inflections are more difficult to interpret than facial expressions, they can clarify the message.

When we write, including writing on social media, our "listeners" do not have any information beyond our words. It becomes extremely important that we choose words that accurately reflect the message we want to send.

It is generally easier to become aggressive without realizing it when we write than when we talk. For one thing, there is no one to stop us. We are not getting any immediate feedback on how our reader is responding. In face to face communication, we have cues from the listener on how our message is being received, and we can modify it as necessary.

When we write, sometimes it is as though we lose our "filter" and say things without realizing the impact the words may have. We can become aggressive without realizing it. It is often a good practice, especially in a heated or stressful situation, to write something, save it, review it the next day, and then decide if you still want to send it. You can always send something later, but you cannot retrieve it once it is sent.

Many people do not realize the importance of another aspect of social media. Once it is posted, it lives forever. Before you post something, there are a few questions you should answer.

- Would you be embarrassed if your parents read it?
  If yes, think twice about posting.
- Would you be embarrassed if this resurfaced ten years from now? If yes or maybe, think again about posting it.
- Would it hurt your job if your employer read it?
  If yes, do not post it.
- Would it hurt your prospects of getting a new job if a potential employer read it? If yes, do not post it. Employers do a great deal of searching on social media to determine what type of person you are before they make a job offer. Sometimes they do this to determine if they even want to interview you.

We need to be aware of all our communication. We need to strive to be assertive in all forms of communication, not passive or aggressive. Remembering rights and respect is the key.

CHAPTER 05

Passive Behavior

RABBITS ARE CUTE and cuddly. Rabbits are also prey. They are eaten. They spend their lives in hiding, venturing out only for food. They have to be on constant alert for potential attack. Their first defense is to freeze and pretend not to exist. When an attack comes, they run, hide, and hope for escape until the next attack.

Rabbits do not have a choice. They are what nature made them.

As human beings, we have choices. We are made to grow, develop, and change as necessary to survive and succeed.

If you do not respect your rights as a person, how can you respect yourself as a person?

In general:

- **People are not going to respect you any more than you respect yourself.**
- **People are not going to treat you any better than you treat yourself.**
- **People are not going to stand up for you if you do not stand up for yourself.**
- **You must respect yourself first, before others will respect you.**

If you do not express your opinions, people will think that even you do not think your opinions are worthwhile. If you do not, why should they? It makes it easy for people to disregard your thoughts and feelings if you are passive and do not speak out.

People are not telepathic. People cannot read our minds. Unless we speak up and tell someone what we think, he/she will not know. "If he/she loved me, he/she would know what I want" is not based in reality. It does not happen. It is not other people's responsibility to try to figure out what we think and feel, either; it is our responsibility to tell them.

We are passive when we do not communicate our thoughts and feelings to others *as appropriate!*

Do not confuse passive with private. Not everything has to be shared, or should be shared, despite what is on social media. The deciding factor is if someone is doing or saying something that is disruptive to your life. If so, then you need to be assertive and talk to that person. If it is not disruptive, then it does not matter if you say something or not.

Sometimes it is better just to let things roll off you like water off a duck's back.

Passive is also different than waiting for the right time and place. Someone may say or do something that you need to address. It might be good to wait until you can discuss it privately, however. Speaking in private is sometimes more respectful than speaking in public. If the "right time" never comes, however, then evaluate if you are being passive and avoiding the issue.

If you complain to others, but not to the person causing you distress, that is still passive behavior. Speaking up is not assertive unless it is to the person who is negatively affecting your life.

Here is a hint that some of you may appreciate. Women have a tendency to end sentences with an upward inflection. This makes the statement sound like a question. This makes us sound uncertain, unsure of ourselves, and passive. Practice ending statements with a downward inflection. It works. It makes us sound more confident and powerful—assertive.

Do you want to live your life passively, like a rabbit? Do you want to live in fear, to hide, and to run away from life?

Remember: The choice is yours!

CHAPTER 06

Costs of Being Passive

THERE ARE, OF course, costs associated with being passive. Costs for you might be different than costs for someone else. Costs depend upon what is important to us. In general, costs relate to how our relationships with others are affected. Another major cost is how we feel about ourselves.

It is difficult for us to feel good about ourselves if we are passive. When we are passive it is as though we do not respect our rights and ourselves. It is hard to have confidence and healthy self-esteem when we are passive. If for no other reason than to feel better about ourselves, it is worthwhile to become more assertive.

Respect and communication are foundation stones of any relationship. Some possible relationship costs related to being passive follow.

▪ Spouse/Partner

If you are passive with your spouse, you cannot have an equal partnership. How can your partnership be equal if you do not contribute to it by stating what you think, by giving your opinion?

If you are passive, you are forcing your partner to try to determine what you think and feel. You are forcing your partner to make all the decisions.

Is this what you really want? Do you want someone running your life for you?

Being passive can lead to resentment, not just from you, but from your partner.

▪ Children

Something very important to remember with children is that they are still developing. They do not have fully formed egos and look to adults for boundaries. They want and need this. If you are passive, they are forced to form their own boundaries, but they do not have the skills or ability to do this.

As a parent, you must set the standard, set the expectation of your children's behavior. Children will try to get away with as much as they can. This is part of their learning process. You cannot be passive and set standards at the same time. You have to be assertive enough to say "no" and stick to it.

You are also the primary role model for your children. Do you want your children to be passive? Do you want your children not to respect their rights? Not to expect others to respect them? To let others walk all over them?

Children learn from observation. "Do as I say and not as I do" does not work. They will learn much more from how you act than by what words you speak.

If you are passive, your children may also learn to be passive. Or they may learn that if they do not have to listen to you, they do not have to listen to anyone.

It is as important for them as it is for you that they respect you. If they do not respect you, do you really think they will listen to you—especially as they get older?

Your children will not always like what you do, but as long as you behave in a manner deserving of respect, it will work.

■ Parents

Depending upon how you were raised, it can be difficult not to be passive with your parents. Many of us were raised with the idea that parents are always right. There will probably come a time, however, when you will need to be assertive and set boundaries.

It is acceptable to disagree with parents. It is acceptable to be assertive with parents. When you are, just be extra careful to treat them with respect. They may be relieved that you have grown up and can stand on your own.

Remember, though, that there are times when family dynamics make this extremely difficult, especially in dysfunctional families. Sometimes the best approach is to seek professional help and support. If you think that maybe you should, then you probably should. Trust your judgment.

■ **Friends**

If you are passive with your friends, some will take advantage of you. If they do, are they really friends? Maybe not. If that is the case, what is the risk in being assertive? The worse that can happen is that you lose a not-really-a-friend.

Others can become frustrated and leave. They may think you do not want to be a friend with them if you do not speak up. They may not like trying to guess how you feel and making the decisions in the friendship.

■ **Supervisors**

This can be another difficult situation. Most of us are dependent upon our supervisor for our livelihood.

Nevertheless, being passive can cause problems. If you take on more work than you can do and do well because you do not want to confront your boss, there will be consequences. If you cannot complete the work, or complete it well, it will affect how you are perceived as a worker. This will affect your performance appraisals and pay increases.

It can also affect your personal life. If you take on too much, and work too much, you will miss doing things in your personal life. This usually involves less time with family and less time for you.

Earlier we discussed that people are not telepathic. Believe it or not, supervisors are human, too, and are not telepathic. If you keep taking on more work without saying anything, your supervisor will continue to give you more work.

■ Employees

If you are passive with your employees, if you show that you do not respect yourself, they will not respect you. If they do not respect you, they will not listen to you. If they do not respect you, they will not do what you say.

Another consideration is that if you will not stand up for yourself with them, they will know that you will never stand up for them if the time comes. You cannot achieve loyalty without respect.

■ Co-workers

The people we work with are often important people in our lives. We may see them more than our families. If you are passive with them, they may try to take advantage of you. They may also decide not to help you if they do not see you as helping yourself.

■ Customers

Dealing with customers can be a very tricky situation. Usually the best thing to do is follow company policy.

If you are passive with customers, they may interpret that to mean that you are not listening and that you do not care. At the very least, you can actively listen to them, take the time to record the details of the situation, let them know you understand how they feel, and tell them what you can do about the situation.

When we are passive, we let others have a great deal of power and control over us. Is that what you want?

Another way to look at it: Would you want to be in a relationship with you? Would you want to be your partner, child, parent, supervisor, employee, co-worker, associate, or friend?

Remember, unlike rabbits, you can choose to grow and develop into the person you want to be. Remember, too, being passive in any situation is a choice. You can choose to change. You can choose to be assertive, not passive.

Another important consideration is that whatever you choose, you, and you alone, are responsible for that choice and the consequences of that choice. If you continue to choose to be passive, there will be costs/consequences. Are you willing to accept responsibility for these consequences? Or do you want to choose to change?

A price I paid for being passive was a friendship. I had a friend throughout most of elementary school and all of high school. After high school graduation, our lives took different turns. I moved away to attend college. She married and had children.

Throughout college, I tried to visit her when I went home to visit my parents. I did not see her each time I went home, but I saw her on a fairly regular basis. I continued this after college and as I started my career.

Gradually my visits became fewer and fewer and finally stopped altogether. The reason? Every time I saw her all she wanted to do was complain about her husband, her children, and her problems. She never seemed interested in what I was doing or what my life was like.

I became tired of making all the effort and having it be all about her. Rather than be assertive and confront her, however, I acted like prey and ran away. That does not sound good, does it? But it is the truth. I was passive. I was a rabbit. The result is that we have lost touch and have not seen each other for many years.

With the benefit of 20/20 hindsight, I realize I should have been assertive. I should have stood up and spoken out. If I had told her how I felt, it would have given her the opportunity to change if she wanted. Plus, I would have the satisfaction of knowing that I tried.

Why did I not do that? It does not seem like such a difficult thing now. But at the time I did not want to confront her. It was easier not to do so. However, easier does not mean better.

The cost? A friendship that probably did not need to end.

It is time for another mental exercise. A table follows. Think of a situation in which you were passive and now wish you had been assertive. Describe:

- Who was involved.
- What the situation was.
- What action you took.
- What the outcome was.
- What you could have done assertively and possible outcomes of that action (you can come back to this after finishing the book if you want).

Write as much detail as you would like. The goal is to start thinking about whether the outcome you achieved was the outcome you desired. If not, would a different action have gotten a better result?

Table 6-1 **Passive Example**
Who
Situation
Action
Outcome
Assertive Option and Possible Outcome

Whenever we are considering change, it can be helpful to look at the total picture. Usually there are:

- **Benefits of remaining the same.**
- **Benefits of changing.**
- **Costs of changing.**
- **Costs of remaining the same.**

Think about the benefits and costs to you of remaining the same and changing. On the following pages, write what you consider to be benefits and costs of remaining the same in general and/or for specific relationships. You may find that your current approach is fine for some relationships, but that you would like to make changes in others.

There are not any right or wrong answers. This exercise is simply to help you decide if you want to make changes, and—if so—where.

Table 6-2	**Benefits to Me of Remaining the Same** (Related to Passive Behavior)
In General	
Spouse/Partner	
Children	
Parents	
Friends	
Supervisor	
Employees	
Co-Workers	
Customers	
Others	

Table 6-3	**Benefits to Me of Changing** (Related to Passive Behavior)
In General	
Spouse/Partner	
Children	
Parents	
Friends	
Supervisor	
Employees	
Co-Workers	
Customers	
Others	

Table 6-4	**Costs to Me of Changing** (Related to Passive Behavior)
In General	
Spouse/Partner	
Children	
Parents	
Friends	
Supervisor	
Employees	
Co-Workers	
Customers	
Others	

DON'T ACT LIKE PREY! · SUSAN L. FARRELL, MBA

Table 6-5	**Costs to Me of Remaining The Same** (Related to Passive Behavior)

In General
Spouse/Partner
Children
Parents
Friends
Supervisor
Employees
Co-Workers
Customers
Others

Change is rarely easy. When we can see the costs and consequences associated with our current behavior, it can help us decide if we want to change. After deciding to change, we need to make a commitment to change.

On the next page, summarize what you will do based upon the thoughts you recorded on the previous pages. Making a commitment to yourself that you *will* take these actions greatly increases the likelihood of your success.

Table 6-6 **Summary of What I Will Do** (Related to Passive Behavior)	
In General	
Spouse/Partner	
Children	
Parents	
Friends	
Supervisor	
Employees	
Co-Workers	
Customers	
Others	

CHAPTER 07

Aggressive Behavior

MOUNTAIN LIONS ARE aggressive. They have to be. They are carnivores. If they do not hunt, they do not eat, and they die.

Mountain lions do not have any more of a choice than rabbits do. Nature made them the way they are.

As human beings, we have choices. Although there are people who kill other people, that is an extreme example of aggressive behavior. There are also those people who prey on other people in various ways. These examples are beyond the scope of this book. If you are in a relationship that is mentally, emotionally, or physically abusive, then you need to seek professional help.

For our purposes in this book, we will define aggressive behavior as treating others with disrespect. This behavior can destroy relationships.

Unfortunately, this can be easy to do. Every time we yell at someone, snap at someone, we are treating him or her with disrespect. We are being aggressive. We are also being aggressive when we do not consider the other's thoughts and feelings, only our own. This is often a very selfish approach.

Others will not respect us if we do not respect them and treat them with respect. We need to remember that their rights are just as important as our rights. People may do what we want out of fear when we are aggressive, but fear does not work the way love or loyalty does.

When we are aggressive, our communication may be one-way. We may tell others what we think, but if we do not listen, we are not really communicating. Communication must be two-way. We do not learn if we do not actively listen to ensure that we understand what the other person is saying.

Also, people will not communicate openly if they are afraid to do so. They will tell us what they think we want to hear, not what we need to hear. There will be many things happening in our professional and personal lives that we will not know. We cannot make good decisions with bad or missing information.

Another issue with aggressive behavior is that often people, like animals, fight back when they feel threatened. If you are aggressive with someone, they may feel that they have to become aggressive, as well, to protect themselves. This can easily escalate an already bad situation.

Do you want to live your life aggressively, like a mountain lion? Do you want to attack those around you and in the process destroy your relationships?

The choice is yours!

CHAPTER 08

Costs of Being Aggressive

THERE ARE, OF course, costs associated with being aggressive. Costs are peculiar to the individual. What is a cost to you may not be to someone else.

Some possible relationship costs related to being aggressive follow.

■ Spouse/Partner

A marriage (or other committed relationship) should be a partnership, ideally an equal partnership. It cannot be if you do not respect the rights of your partner.

If you are aggressive with your spouse or partner, what is going to keep him or her in the relationship? Why should he or she stay? Would you if the roles were reversed?

■ Children

Various negative things can happen when you are aggressive with your children, when you treat them with disrespect.

If they see you, their primary role model, as being aggressive, they may also become aggressive. If their rights are not respected, why should they respect the rights of others? They may take the behavior they see at home to school and into the neighborhood.

If they are not treated with respect, it can affect their self-confidence and self-esteem. They may believe they do not deserve to be treated any better.

If you are aggressive with them and always tell them what to do, they can become dependent on that and never learn to think for themselves.

They may fear you. They may do what you say when they are young and rebel when they get older. Compliance out of fear is not compliance.

Would any of this be the relationship you want with your children?

■ Parents

Relationships with parents can be difficult and challenging sometimes, especially as our parents age and we move into being the care-givers instead of the care-receivers. Keep in mind that the situation is also difficult for them.

As discussed before, it is acceptable to set boundaries. Just do it in an assertive way, with respect, without going into aggressive behavior. Even if you do not like how your parents raised you, they probably did the best they knew how and deserve your respect for trying.

Also remember that it is acceptable to seek professional help. Very complicated emotions can arise that may require assistance to resolve.

▪ Friends

If you are aggressive with your friends, are you sure they actually consider you a friend? What is in it for them? Do they continue to stay friends because they like you or for other reasons?

If you are aggressive (disrespectful), how long do you think your real friends will tolerate that behavior?

▪ Supervisor

Your supervisor can do many things if he/she does not think you are treating him/her with respect. Repercussions can include poor performance appraisals, lack of pay increases, no promotions, and even dismissal.

Some supervisors leave a great deal to be desired. If it is not possible to respect the person, at least respect the position.

▪ Employees

Studies have shown that the primary reason employees leave a job is because of their immediate supervisor. If you treat your employees disrespectfully, the good ones will leave. The ones that will stay are those that cannot get a job anywhere else.

Employees may do what you tell them out of fear. That does not create the same results as a working relationship based on respect and trust. If you treat your employees with respect, they are more likely to respect you. If they do, they are more likely to work well whether you are there or not. Which working environment would you rather create?

■ Co-Workers

If you treat your co-workers with disrespect, some may just avoid you. Some may try to retaliate and sabotage you. It is a likely prospect that they will not support or assist you.

■ Customers

Some customers are very difficult. They can be rude and obnoxious. It can be difficult sometimes not to become aggressive. However, customers deserve to be treated with respect. They are, after all, the ones providing the money for your paycheck. If you do become aggressive, you will probably pay a much higher price, perhaps your job, than the customer will. Keep in mind that the person is probably frustrated with the situation, not you as a person, so try not to take it personally.

When we are aggressive, we are disrespectful toward others. We forget that they have the same rights we do. This hurts our relationships. Ultimately, it hurts us as much as the people around us.

As discussed with passive behavior, if you are aggressive, would you want to be in a relationship with you? Would you want to be your partner, child, parent, supervisor, employee, co-worker, associate, or friend?

Remember, unlike mountain lions, you can choose to grow and develop into the person you want to be. Remember, too, being aggressive in any situation is a choice. You can choose to change. You can choose to be assertive, not aggressive.

Again, whatever you choose, you, and you alone, are responsible for that choice and the consequences of that choice. If you continue to choose to be aggressive, there will be costs/consequences. Are you willing to accept responsibility for these costs? Or do you want to choose to change?

People do notice when we are being aggressive. They may not say anything, but they notice. For example, when I get hungry, I get irritable. I usually take early lunches because of this.

I had a wonderful administrative assistant in a previous position. She would often help out on another floor of the building, so if I could not tell her I was going to lunch I would call her so she would know where I was. One day I was really involved with a project and it was almost 2:00 before I could take lunch. I called to let her know. Her response: "What! You haven't eaten yet? There's no one dead up there, is there? Do I have to clean up any blood?"

I knew she was joking, but it made me realize that other people do recognize when we are being aggressive even if we do not. Not everyone will handle it with humor, either.

Since that incident, I have tried very hard to determine why I slip into aggressive behavior. Is it really another person who is causing it? Is it the situation? Or is it something unrelated, such as hunger and a drop in blood sugar? Regardless of what is causing it, is it fair to take it out on the person who happens to be there? No.

In addition to being aware of low blood sugar, I also try to have a plan to deal with it. I carry snacks with me. It helps. It may not resolve what is going on around me, but it helps what is going on inside of me. I can then handle any situation more appropriately. I have also found that sometimes the best thing to do is to step away, clear my head, and then resume.

Another trend I have noticed is that sometimes I wait too long to say something. By the time I do say something, it has had too long to brew inside me. Rather than calmly state the issue, I sometimes overreact and cross from being assertive to being aggressive. I sometimes do this when I am angry.

Recognizing these trends helps in controlling them. It makes it easy to take a deep breath and think about how I am going to say something as well as what to say.

Recognizing your trends, or your triggers, may help you stay on the assertive side of the line rather than cross over into the aggressive side.

We are all in situations sometimes in which despite our best efforts we become aggressive and disrespectful of someone else. When this happens, sometimes apologizing can make a tremendous difference.

One time I was in Cleveland for a speaking engagement. The return trip to Milwaukee that evening was horrible. My flight from Cleveland to Chicago was delayed because of weather in Chicago. When I finally arrived in Chicago, I found that my flight to Milwaukee was also delayed. Later it was

DON'T ACT LIKE PREY! · SUSAN L. FARRELL, MBA

delayed again. And again. At one point the gate attendant announced that, although the flight was not cancelled, if anyone wanted to reschedule for the next day they could (not a good sign). At some point after that, she announced that anyone who wanted to take the last bus from Chicago to Milwaukee could trade their plane ticket for a bus ticket (really not a good sign).

Like everyone else, I went up to the counter to try to find out whether the plane was ever going to leave or not. I was frustrated, tired, irritated, and started snapping at her. I caught myself, took a deep breath, and apologized: "I am sorry. This is not your fault. You are doing what you can. I am sorry for taking my frustration out on you."

Not only was she very gracious about it, but she helped me later. I finally decided to take a limo back to Milwaukee. She patiently explained what would happen with my luggage, where to find the limos, and what to do. She was extremely nice. I doubt I would have received that treatment had I not apologized.

When we are aggressive, sometimes the best we can do is apologize.

A table follows. Think of a situation in which you were aggressive and now wish you had been assertive. Describe:

- Who was involved.
- What the situation was.
- What action you took.
- What the outcome was.
- What you could have done assertively and possible outcomes of that action (you can come back to this after finishing the book if you want).

Write as much detail as you would like. The goal is to start thinking about whether the outcome you achieved was the outcome you desired. If not, would a different action have gotten a better result?

Table 8-1	**Aggressive Example**
Who	
Situation	
Action	
Outcome	
Assertive Option and Possible Outcome	

As we discussed with passive behavior, whenever we are considering change, it can be helpful to look at the total picture. Usually there are:

- Benefits of remaining the same.
- Benefits of changing.
- Costs of changing.
- Costs of remaining the same.

Again, think about the benefits and costs to you of remaining the same and changing related to aggressive behavior. On the following pages, write what you consider to be benefits and costs of remaining the same in general and/ or for specific relationships. You may find that your current approach is fine for some relationships, but that you would like to make changes in others.

Remember, there are not any right or wrong answers. This exercise is simply to help you decide if you want to make changes, and—if so—where.

Table 8-2	**Benefits to Me of Remaining the Same** (Related to Aggressive Behavior)
In General	
Spouse/Partner	
Children	
Parents	
Friends	
Supervisor	
Employees	
Co-Workers	
Customers	
Others	

COSTS OF BEING AGGRESSIVE

Table 8-3	**Benefits to Me of Changing** (Related to Aggressive Behavior)
In General	
Spouse/Partner	
Children	
Parents	
Friends	
Supervisor	
Employees	
Co-Workers	
Customers	
Others	

    DON'T ACT LIKE PREY! · SUSAN L. FARRELL, MBA

Table 8-4	**Costs to Me of Changing** (Related to Aggressive Behavior)
In General	
Spouse/Partner	
Children	
Parents	
Friends	
Supervisor	
Employees	
Co-Workers	
Customers	
Others	

Table 8-5	**Costs to Me of Remaining the Same** (Related to Aggressive Behavior)
In General	
Spouse/Partner	
Children	
Parents	
Friends	
Supervisor	
Employees	
Co-Workers	
Customers	
Others	

As discussed before, change is rarely easy. When we can see the costs and consequences associated with our current behavior, however, it can help us decide if we want to change. After deciding to change, we need to make a commitment to change.

On the next page, summarize what you will do based upon the thoughts you recorded on the previous pages. Making a commitment to yourself that you *will* take these actions greatly increases the likelihood of your success.

COSTS OF BEING AGGRESSIVE

Table 8-6 **Summary of What I Will Do** (Related to Aggressive Behavior)
In General
Spouse/Partner
Children
Parents
Friends
Supervisor
Employees
Co-Workers
Customers
Others

CHAPTER 09

Assertive Behavior

THE AMERICAN BLACK bear is a good example of an assertive animal. (Do not confuse a black bear with a grizzly bear. Grizzlies are predators and very aggressive.)

Black bears do not prey on other animals. They eat primarily vegetation, including berries. Although they do eat insects and sometimes rodents, they are not predators like mountain lions.

If attacked or threatened, a black bear will stand up for itself and fight. If it does not feel threatened, it will leave others alone.

Like rabbits and mountain lions, the black bear is what nature made it. It does not have a choice.

As human beings, we can always choose our behavior.

When we are assertive, we communicate our thoughts and feelings to others as appropriate. We stand up for ourselves. We do not let others take advantage of us. We respect our rights and balance this with respecting the rights of others.

Being assertive is one of the most important strategies for professional and personal success. It is not enough that we are assertive in one aspect of our lives; we need to be assertive in all aspects of our lives.

This can seem difficult to do, until we remember that it is really all about respecting rights, our rights and the rights of others. We respect others and ourselves.

Assertive communication is necessary for authentic relationships. Assertive communication starts with respecting your own thoughts and feelings. Once you truly respect your right to have those thoughts and feelings, it becomes easier to share them with others. This can take you from passive to assertive.

If you remember that others have the same rights you do, and respect those rights, it becomes easier to communicate assertively without becoming aggressive. Remember to listen as well as speak. Active listening is key to good communication.

Remember, just as you can choose to be passive or aggressive, you can choose to be assertive!

CHAPTER 10

Benefits of Being Assertive

AS THERE ARE costs with being passive or aggressive, there are benefits to being assertive.

The first time I presented this information at a conference, I asked the participants what they thought a benefit to being assertive was. One woman said, "You just might get what you want." That sums it up. The best way to get what you want is to start by asking for it.

Other possible benefits follow. Your benefits may be different. These are provided to provoke your thinking.

■ Spouse/Partner

You have a much better chance of having an equal partnership if you are assertive in the relationship. Of course, your partner needs to be assertive, as well. If one person is assertive, though, it makes it easier for the other one to be assertive.

Being assertive greatly increases your chances of having the relationship you want.

▪ Children

You become an excellent role model to your children on how to be assertive. This will help them as children and when they become adults. If they are already adults, maybe they could still benefit from a great role model.

Where we have discussed children in this book, keep in mind that it does not mean just the children that you raise. It can also mean grandchildren, nieces, nephews, and other children in your life. Sometimes we have a much greater impact on all the children in our lives than we realize. This can be especially important when their home life leaves something to be desired.

▪ Parents

When we are assertive with our parents, it helps move the parent-child relationship to an adult-adult relationship. Yes, they will always be our parents and we will always be their children. However, that relationship can grow and develop. Being assertive will help with that growth.

When you are assertive, you can set boundaries with your parents, if needed, in such a way that they know you still love and respect them.

Family dynamics can complicate matters greatly. Sometimes the assertive approach in dealing with significant others, parents, children, and other family members is to seek professional assistance in dealing with the situation.

Friends

Perhaps the best thing about being assertive with your friends is that you know who your friends really are. You know that they stay with you because they value your friendship.

Supervisor

If you are assertive with your supervisor, you will probably gain his/her respect. When that happens, provided you are doing your job and doing it well, you are more likely to receive the recognition you want. Recognition may be through awards, pay increases, or promotions.

Employees

If you treat your employees with respect, they will be more likely to respect you in return. They may not like everything you need them to do, but they will be more likely to do it if they respect you. You may see an improvement in their work and productivity.

Co-Workers

We spend a great deal of time with co-workers. The better relationships that we have with them, the more enjoyable our lives will be. Treating them with respect is the best first step to having them treat us with respect.

Customers

As mentioned before, it is important to follow company policy. Depending upon the situation, assertiveness might be solving the problem for the customer. If the problem cannot be solved to the customer's satisfaction, assertiveness might be to actively listen, diffuse the situation, and do what you can. Sometimes the best approach is to turn it over to your supervisor. Or, if a supervisor is not present, the assertive approach might be to report the situation later and learn what to do next time.

The key to assertiveness is to express yourself with tact, thoughtfulness, professionalism, and consideration. This demonstrates that you respect yourself and the other person.

If you were assertive, not passive or aggressive, think how enjoyable it would be to be in a relationship with you! And all the relationships that you are in would probably be more enjoyable for you.

Although the black bear is naturally assertive, maybe you are not. Remember, though, you can choose to grow and develop into the person you want to be even if it does not come naturally. It is a choice that only you can make.

Again, whatever you choose, you, and you alone, are responsible for that choice and the consequences of that choice. If you choose to be assertive, the consequences are usually benefits. They are usually positive.

I would like to provide you with some examples of assertive behavior. None is a perfect example, but at least I stood up and spoke out on my behalf.

Seventh grade was full of changes. My class of about 10 went from a rural elementary school to the middle school in town. From staying in the same classroom with two grades and one teacher per room, we went to a school where the teachers stayed in the same rooms and the students moved. We were also with students from all over the county.

It was fun and at the same time a little scary to be meeting so many new people and making new friends.

One day, a few girls I was friends with said that if I wanted to continue to be friends with another group of girls, then they did not want to be friends with me anymore. I do not remember the details as to why. It could not have been that dramatic.

I do remember, though, becoming extremely angry. How dare they try to tell me whom I could have as friends! What gave them the right to dictate to me what I could do and not do?! In typical pre-teen fashion I told them that I did not want them as friends, either, and stormed off. I spoke to only one of the girls again, and that was a few years later.

If a similar situation happened today, I would handle it better. I would try to determine what the problem really was and make the solution more of a win-win. Considering my age at the time, though, I am proud that I stood up and spoke out. I was assertive. I did not let them control me. I did not act like prey. I did not act like a predator, either. I did not attack them. I did not yell or call names or hit anyone. I was assertive.

A long time ago, I had a boss (a woman) whose boss (a man) was very much a micro-manager. One of the results was that she did not give me my performance appraisals; he did.

One year she came back to our office ranting and raving after receiving her performance appraisal. She had gotten only a small fraction of the possible increase, and she was understandably upset. Unfortunately, salary increases from her boss were related to politics, not performance.

She said she had told him exactly what she thought. I did not say anything, but I knew that was a mistake. He was one of those people who always had to be right, and everything had to be his idea. I also knew that if she received only a very small increase, so would I. My performance appraisal was next.

I was correct in that he gave me the same small increase. I did not know what to do. I knew ranting and raving would not do any good. But I did not want to just accept it, either. By the time the performance appraisal was over I still did not have a plan. I left and thought about it some more.

By the next day I had a plan. I asked to meet with him. He agreed. I asked him a simple question: "What do I have to do differently next year to get the full increase?" And then I sat quietly and looked at him. He looked at me. He looked around his office. He looked at me again. I continued to keep my mouth shut. He looked around the office some more. I continued to stay quiet, forcing him to say something.

After several minutes he said he could not think of anything I could do differently. I thanked him for his time and left his office.

I thought about demanding that he give me the full percentage increase. I also knew I would not win that battle.

I knew he would come up with excuses and that if I went to someone in the human resources department, he would find a way to get back at me. I decided to lose a battle in hopes of winning the war.

I did win the war. Every year after that, I received the full percentage increase allowed for my position.

One point I want to make here is that being aggressive usually does not work, at least in the long run. My supervisor was aggressive. She said what she thought without showing any respect for her supervisor, or at least showing respect for his position. I did not respect him as a person, either, but when I met with him I still treated him with respect because of his position. I think that helped me. I know that her reaction did not help her during the rest of her time with the company.

Another point is that it is sometimes acceptable to be passive at first, until you can go back with an assertive plan. Never be afraid to go back after you have had a chance to think about it. Rarely is it too late.

Some of you may think that I was too assertive or not assertive enough. Each person is different, and each situation is different. What matters is whether you are happy with the result you achieved. I was. I still think this was as good as I could expect considering the situation and the participants.

Once upon a time, I had a supervisor who lied. Not only did she lie, but she expected her employees to lie for her. I discovered the first part early in my employment. I decided I could tolerate it, even though it went against one of my basic values. I never imagined the second part existed until the day she asked me to lie to a customer for her.

I was shocked! I had never had anyone ask me to lie for them before. I was so shocked that I did it. I have regretted it ever since. I was passive, but I had no idea how to be assertive in this situation, and there was not enough time to think of a plan.

After she asked me to lie again, I decided I was not going to do it. I did not tell her that, though. I was still not at the assertive stage. I still wanted and needed my job. Fortunately, the situation that she anticipated did not happen, and, therefore, I was able to avoid confronting her.

By the third time she asked me to lie (this occurred over several months), I was ready. I still wanted my job, but I had a plan if I lost it. I did not want to sacrifice one of my most important values for her. When she asked me to lie to a customer again, I simply looked at her and said, "No. I am not going to lie."

She looked at me as though she could not believe anyone would say that to her. Then she started backtracking, stated that that was not what she meant, and left my office.

The situation was scary! I thought she might fire me on the spot (although I had already decided to fight it if she did). Yet I think I handled it well. I stood up to her, and, more importantly, I stood up for my values. I stated that I was not going to lie, but I did not become aggressive. I spoke with respect. I did not yell, rant, or rave. I did not make threats. I was assertive.

In some situations, we may need time to become assertive. We may need to be passive until we can reach the stage when it is possible to be assertive. We may also need to develop a back-up plan. That is fine. We can wait until we are ready, as long as we do become ready, or decide to live with the situation.

I would like to share one more assertiveness story. This is a personal rather than a professional story. It is not that easy to tell, but I think it demonstrates the need to set boundaries and then defend them.

In the fall of 2008, my husband and I visited my parents for the weekend. They lived on the farm where my father was born and lived his entire life. (The land was no longer farmed, but my brothers and I owned the land and buildings.) During the visit, I told my parents that I had decided to leave a part-time position I had so that I could focus full time on my speaking career. They were both supportive of my decision.

A few weeks later, Dad passed away from a heart attack. My brothers and I knew that Mom could not live alone in the country, largely because she could not drive. Although she had some trouble walking, she was capable of living on her own. Mom also knew this. We discussed options such as senior apartments in town and started investigating.

I thought we were all in agreement until out of the blue Mom said, "Susan, since you are not working now, you can come take care of me."

In shock I blurted out, "But I am working. Remember, I left the part-time job so that I could work full-time on my business." I think my tone was assertive, not aggressive. My main thought was that I could not spend three hours on the road, one way, to take care of her and still have a professional life. Especially since she could do almost everything on her own.

"Oh, yes." That was all she said.

We were able to find a lovely senior apartment complex in town. A long-time family friend also lived there, which made it even nicer.

And yet Mom kept pushing that I needed to regularly drive three hours to do things for her and then drive three hours back to my own home. Instead, I found community resources that she could use, such as a driver to take her shopping. For some things there were not any good options, such as taking her cat to the vet or talking with the doctor about test results. Those I did. (My brothers and extended family members also helped significantly with those things that they could.)

After my saying, "No" quite a bit, Mom started finding resources on her own. She found a local grocery store that delivered to the apartment building once a week. All she had to do was call in her order. She found someone to clean her apartment when she decided she did not want to do that anymore.

Mom had the right to ask for what she wanted. I also had the right not to agree to it.

It was difficult to set and then defend the boundary that I was not going to give up my life to do the things for my mother that she could, directly or indirectly, do for herself. I am extremely glad that I did set and defend this boundary, though. My life is better because of it, and I think my mother's is, too. She has maintained a higher level of independence, and that is good.

On the following page is a table, similar to two of the others. This time, think of a situation when you were assertive. Describe:

- Who was involved.
- What the situation was.
- What action you took.
- What the outcome was.

Was the outcome of this situation better than the outcomes when you were passive or aggressive?

Table 10-1 **Assertive Example**
Who
Situation
Action
Outcome

DON'T ACT LIKE PREY! · SUSAN L. FARRELL, MBA

As we discussed with passive and aggressive behavior, whenever we are considering change, it can be helpful to look at the total picture. Usually there are:

- **Benefits of remaining the same.**
- **Benefits of changing.**
- **Costs of changing.**
- **Costs of remaining the same.**

Again, think about the benefits and costs to you of remaining the same and changing related to assertive behavior. There may be costs with changing. Are there any hidden reasons why you do not want to change? Are there more obvious reasons? If you become assertive, you will have to take responsibility for your choice. Can your self-esteem handle that? If you are in a dysfunctional relationship, becoming assertive may mean that you lose that relationship. Are you ready for that?

As you did with passive and aggressive behavior, on the following pages, write what you consider to be benefits and costs of remaining the same in general and/or for specific relationships. What you think are costs and benefits may be very different from the examples given here. And that is good. Everyone is different. What is important is what you think.

Remember, as with the other tables, there are not any right or wrong answers. This exercise is simply to help you decide if you want to make changes, and—if so—where.

Table 10-2 **Benefits to Me of Remaining the Same** (Related to Assertive Behavior)
In General
Spouse/Partner
Children
Parents
Friends
Supervisor
Employees
Co-Workers
Customers
Others

DON'T ACT LIKE PREY! · SUSAN L. FARRELL, MBA

Table 10-3	**Benefits to Me of Changing** (Related to Assertive Behavior)
In General	
Spouse/Partner	
Children	
Parents	
Friends	
Supervisor	
Employees	
Co-Workers	
Customers	
Others	

Table 10-4 **Costs of Me Changing** (Related to Assertive Behavior)
In General
Spouse/Partner
Children
Parents
Friends
Supervisor
Employees
Co-Workers
Customers
Others

DON'T ACT LIKE PREY! · SUSAN L. FARRELL, MBA

Table 10-5	**Costs of Me Remaining the Same** (Related to Assertive Behavior)
In General	
Spouse/Partner	
Children	
Parents	
Friends	
Supervisor	
Employees	
Co-Workers	
Customers	
Others	

People have a tendency to do things to avoid pain or gain pleasure. Both can motivate us to change. Think about what pain you could avoid by making changes and what pleasure you could gain by making changes. How could your life be better by changing?

On the next page, summarize what you *will* do based upon the thoughts you recorded on the previous pages. You may want to review what you wrote in the previous exercises and make one final commitment page. This also becomes your action plan.

Table 10-6 **Summary of What I Will Do** (Related to Assertive Behavior)
In General
Spouse/Partner
Children
Parents
Friends
Supervisor
Employees
Co-Workers
Customers
Others

CHAPTER 11

Conclusion

WE HAVE BEEN discussing passive, aggressive, and assertive behavior in rather simplistic terms. This is to help you think about your own behaviors, which ones you would like to keep and which ones you would like to change.

Please keep in mind that assertiveness looks different from culture to culture, situation to situation, and person to person. Even treating someone with respect can look different in different cultures. It can look different just based upon how you were raised. There are people who grew up where yelling at each other, for example, is common. Others were raised to believe that yelling is extremely disrespectful.

People may interpret what you do or say as either passive or aggressive when you meant to be assertive. Conversely, you may be interpreting their words and actions as passive or aggressive when they think they are being assertive.

Be aware of this. Listen and observe. If you are not certain if you are interpreting something correctly, ask. If you think the other person has misinterpreted what you meant, question it. Communicating is sometimes the best assertive approach we can take.

When you are dealing with people, your level of assertiveness will probably vary depending upon the situation and/or the person. This is normal. Some people you need to deal with more directly than others. With some people you may need to take a more delicate approach. Be aware of the boundaries in that particular relationship.

If you would like to be more assertive in your relationships, here are some questions to ask yourself. The answers, in addition to the exercises in the book, may help you determine whether you want to change and how.

- **Would you want to be in a relationship (personal or professional) with you?**
- **Why?**
- **Why do you act passively? Aggressively?**
- **Do you want to change?**
- **Why?**

Key points to remember include:

- **Assertive behavior is about respecting yourself and your rights while respecting others and their rights.**
- **Express yourself with tact, thoughtfulness, professionalism, and consideration.**

- Changing yourself takes time. There is a learning process involved. If you are trying, trust yourself that you will learn and change.
- You, and you alone, are responsible for your choices and the consequences of these choices.

A final story I would like to share with you involves an encounter my husband and I had with a black bear in Kenai National Park in Alaska. Despite my knowing what to do when meeting a bear, everything I learned escaped from my brain when Rick and I rounded a turn on the trail and saw a black bear just off the trail ahead of us.

Rick and I both stopped. Rick calmly started taking pictures of the bear. I froze. Rick reminded me that we were supposed to talk to the bear. Right! "Hello, Mr. Bear! Nice day, Mr. Bear! Those look like great berries! Oh, no, Mr. Bear! We don't want any of your berries! We are just out for a hike!" Imagine my saying that in about three nanoseconds and continuing on like that for several minutes. I have no idea what I really said.

When the bear went back to eating berries, Rick and I slowly advanced. Had we retreated and gone down the trail the way we came, when the trail curved, it would have put us beneath the bear on the mountainside. We must have passed it earlier without seeing it. Advancing seemed a better option, as the trail would take us away from the bear.

When the bear stopped eating berries to watch us, Rick and I stopped and watched it. Slowly the bear moved downhill eating berries, and slowly Rick and I advanced uphill on the trail. I continued to babble non-stop. This starting and stopping continued for some time before we were around another bend in the trail and well away from the bear.

The good news: I was assertive with the bear. The bad news: It was not pretty. I was nervous, a little scared, and a little excited. I did not handle the situation as well as I would have liked. However, I stood my ground. I did not run like prey. And I did not hide behind Rick.

Later, when I was reflecting on the incident, I realized that I was assertive with a black bear, in the bear's territory! If I could do that, there was no reason I could not stand up, speak out, and be assertive with people as needed.

The important thing is that we are assertive, that we do stand up for ourselves, that we do speak out on our behalf. We do not have to be great at it; we do not even have to be good at it, at least at first. It is enough that we do it!

**When faced with a difficult situation in which
you know the right thing to do is to be assertive:
*Don't Act Like Prey!***

Author's Note

I WOULD LOVE to see a second edition of this book filled with stories from readers on their experiences with passive, aggressive, and assertive behavior.

If you have a story that you would like to share, please email it to me at **susan@susanlfarrell.com**.

I would also like to know what you liked about the book and if there was anything you did not like about the book. I am constantly trying to improve myself and my work. Your comments, for a second edition of this book and for other books, would be greatly appreciated.

For additional copies of this book, please order through Amazon.com. Or, you can order through my website, **susanlfarrell.com**, and receive a *free* bonus chapter. The bonus chapter will be emailed to you.

As mentioned in the "About the Author" section, I speak nationally on personal leadership for women. If this is a topic that would benefit you, your organization, or any professional associations of which you are a member, please contact me at **susan@susanlfarrell.com**. Also, please go to my website, **susanlfarrell.com**, for additional information.

Thank you, and best to you in your journey to being consistently assertive!

Susan L. Farrell

Acknowledgements

I WOULD LIKE to thank Pat Olson, my cousin and the sister I never had, for her support and understanding throughout my life. She is also one awesome copyeditor and proofreader. This book is much better because of her.

I would like to thank Amy Gurka for agreeing to be content editor for this book. She gave me wonderful ideas and insights which I was delighted and grateful to incorporate. I would also like to thank her for the fantastic foreword for this book.

I would like to thank Andrew Welyczko for designing the cover and interior of the book. He took a bland looking manuscript and made it shine.

I would like to thank all my friends at the Wisconsin Chapter of the National Speakers Association. Without the support and encouragement of so many, I am not sure I would have had the courage to finish and publish this book. You are an inspiration to me.

I would like to thank my parents, Norman and Leola Farrell, for so many things, but especially for teaching me the right values. I think Dad would be proud that his thirst for knowledge has led to a published book.

Finally, I suppose I should thank my brothers. Without any of us realizing it, they probably helped teach me as a child not to show fear, not to act like prey. If I had, I am convinced I would have found an abundance of bugs, snakes, and other critters in my bed and dresser drawers on a regular basis.

About the Author

Susan has always loved to learn. She was one of those geeky kids who liked school and looked forward to starting each new school year. Her love of learning has continued throughout her life. Her learning has occurred not only through formal education but also through lessons learned from personal and professional life experiences. She is also an avid reader.

A normal extension of a love of learning is a love of teaching. Susan has accomplished this in various positions through teaching and training her employees, co-workers, associates, and customers. She has taught as an adjunct instructor at business colleges. She has also informally coached employees, associates, and friends in advancing professionally and personally.

Susan speaks nationally on personal leadership for women. She has more than 25 years of management, consulting, and training experience, including owning her own business, SLF Consulting & Training. She has been speaking nationally for more than 10 years and is a professional member of the National Speakers Association. Her speaking style is clear, concise, and features fun and insightful anecdotes. She has the ability to truly connect with her audience.

Don't Act Like Prey! is Susan's first book. She is inordinately pleased with the opportunity to share her message with an even larger audience.

To contact Susan, please visit her website, **susanlfarrell. com**, or email her at **susan@susanlfarrell.com**.

Made in the USA
Charleston, SC
01 November 2013